Stay At Home, Mom

Even if You're
Single!

Other Titles:

Stay At Home, Mom

Even if You're Single!

Annie Jean Brewer

STAY AT HOME, MOM
EVEN IF YOU'RE SINGLE!

FIRST PRINT EDITION

Note:

This book is not just about moms; it is about anyone raising a family who wants to spend more time with them. I refer to moms in this book because they are the largest demographic currently raising children solo but this book can also be used by couples, single dads, grandparents, or anyone else interested in working from home.

To the children who wish their working parents were able to be at home for them. I hope this helps your dream come true.

Table of Contents

Introduction

Being a stay at home mom (SAHM) is a challenge in this 2-income world. For the *single* parent it can seem almost impossible. How in Heaven's name can one be at home with the kids and still pay the bills?

Thanks to modern technology and a global workplace it is not only possible, it isn't very hard to do. Except for a brief job I took out of boredom I have worked from home since 2008. I have supported my daughter as a single stay at home mother with passive income (I'll explain this term in a bit) from my blog and book sales alone for over a year now. Before that I supported us through freelance work, telecommuting positions and even a computer repair business.

These days I don't really *have* to work; I take days and sometimes weeks off to enjoy the weather or to hang out with my kid. Once I removed the necessity to work it became enjoyable so now I write because I love what I do.

Anyone can do this; it doesn't take any special skills or education. I have little more than a high school diploma[1] myself. Regardless of your education level YOU can do this too! *You* actually have an edge over your fellow parents. How? You are reading this book. That demonstrates that you have a strong desire to improve your life and that you are willing to learn, grow and do what it takes to make it happen.

Within these pages you will find the same method I used to become a single stay at home mom with an income that arrives every month whether I do anything or not. I know that your personality and situation may be different so I am going to offer some options for you to consider but the focus of this book will be on the area that I know best; that of selling information.

Information is an incredible resource; all of us have specialized knowledge that we can share with others who are seeking to learn. Thanks to the blessing of the Internet we can multiply our ability to share this knowledge and create a living wage for ourselves.

Note that this is *not* a get-rich-quick book. While I was able to generate as much money as I wanted through active income (I'll explain this term a bit later as well), it took slightly over a

---

[1] http://annienygma.com/about-me/

year for me to feel comfortable transitioning to the passive income of book sales. I won't tell you how to cheat the system; I offer you a failure-proof method you can use to generate enough income to stay at home with your kids.

This book is my response to my daughter's friends who confided in me that they wish *their* parents would stay at home instead of work all the time. It is to these children, the ones who miss their working parents, that I dedicate this book. I hope that the knowledge within helps more children keep their parents at home.

Review Request

If this book helps you in any way can you please leave a review on your website of choice? This will help others decide if this book is the one they are looking for. I will be happy to send you a PDF copy of this book to read on your computer or share with a friend as a thank you gift for your trouble.

I appreciate you!

Annienyyma

Questions

I'm sure you have many questions; I'll try to answer many of them now so that you can decide if being a stay at home mom (SAHM) is for you.

What are the benefits of being a SAHM?

For one, you get to be the one that watches your children grow up and reach those once-in-a-lifetime milestones. You get to be the one your child bonds with because you are always there. Also (if your child is preschool-age) you will have almost complete control of the most important part of your child's developmental period. You will know what your child has been exposed to because you will have been there.

You won't have to worry about finding a babysitter if your child is sick or worry that your babysitter is molesting your child. You will never have to worry that your child is being abused because you will be there to stop it if something goes too far.

You will be the one your child celebrates with when he is happy and snuggles up to when he is sad.

The best part is that, no matter what happens in your romantic relationships you will be able to provide for your family if there isn't a significant other in your life. If your mate ever looks at you and tells you to get out, you can pack up your stuff and go, knowing that you have money of your own he can't take away!

If your mate ever abuses you or your children you won't be trapped; you will have enough money (and the freedom that only money can buy) to get your own place and make them take a hike!

How do you know so much about being a SAHM?

It was my goal to be a SAHM with all of my children. I worked toward this goal for many years and finally figured out how to accomplish it with my youngest daughter. I started providing for us by working entirely from home in 2008. Before that I combined working at home with part-time positions in restaurants and other places. In 2011 I ran the numbers and realized that we could live on my ebook royalties alone so I stopped pursuing active income entirely.

Since then I have written several more books, hung out with my kid and just enjoyed life. I have no plans to go back into the traditional workforce even after my daughter turns 18 and consider myself fortunate because I won't have to!

Can I become a SAHM without an education?

If you are intelligent enough to read this and apply the information within you DEFINITELY have enough smarts and education to become a SAHM.

I've attempted college more than once without success yet I've been able to provide for us without ANY assistance from a boyfriend for over a decade. For many years I ran a computer repair business out of my home and now I run a successful website, have written 18 books to date and have several more in progress.

If I can accomplish this then you can too! Henry Ford, Bill Gates and Steve Jobs weren't college graduates yet they managed to create huge fortunes so don't let anyone tell you that you aren't smart enough or that you don't have enough education.

There are many types of education. Self-education is the best because you only learn what you need, when you need it. If you weren't self-educated (or interested in self-education) you wouldn't be reading this book. Any attempt to improve your life results in education.

How much money can I make?

How much money you make is limited by you and the time you are willing to invest. *Remember*: If you never get started you will never earn a penny! With a bit of effort it is not impossible to earn several thousand dollars a month in active income. I have one friend who routinely earns $3000+ a month by writing articles online and I used to write enough to earn $1,000-$2,000 a month when I wanted. I would set an earnings goal and reward myself by taking the rest of the month off when I reached it.

With passive income your first payments may be small or they may surprise you. The first week after I published my book The Minimalist Cleaning Method I received around $100 from sales on my blog alone. When I expanded distribution to Amazon, Smashwords, Barnes and Noble, Apple and other retailers my sales went up from there. Also, the more books you publish the more "hooks" you bait in the sea of internet income. More hooks=more money as more shoppers will potentially find your product.

I have friends who are making several thousand dollars a month with ebooks alone. Amanda Hocking and John Locke both have earned over a million dollars with ebook sales. I personally doubled my income in the past year with just a little bit of effort and I have lived exclusively on my book royalties for over a year now. As with many things, you will get out of it what you are willing to put into it but there is no "glass ceiling" or income cap when you build passive income.

How can I earn money as a SAHM?

There are a variety of ways to earn money as a SAHM. It depends upon whether you prefer active income (work for immediate pay) or passive income (doing something once and getting paid over and over). I will cover these different forms of income in a later section.

Where can I work?

While there are small businesses that may allow you to bring your children to work with you, your best bet is to work out of your own home. You have the most freedom with your schedule when you are the one in charge of it. You can take charge of your schedule by doing freelance work (online or offline) or by starting your own business.

You will need a place set aside to work and keep your tools, especially if you have small kids that like to borrow your stuff. In the past I placed a desk in a quiet area of my home (as quiet as possible, anyway) that was off limits to the kids. As they grew older and I became financially able to work when, if and where I wanted this was simplified down to a laptop and a backpack. I keep the backpack positioned on the back of whatever chair I'm sitting in and my laptop on the table. When I'm done I place everything in the backpack and put it away. You don't need a lot of stuff when you are selling the information in your head. ☺

With the right income method you can literally work from anywhere you want to. While some forms of passive income (recording music or videos, for instance) may require you to work in certain conditions (quiet, using particular equipment, etc.) other forms allow you much more freedom. For instance, I have written several books camped out in the back of my van while traveling, on break at a public job, hanging out in restaurants, at the library, in coffee shops, sitting underneath shade trees in the park and even while sitting in the bathtub with my laptop positioned nearby (I didn't get much done for fear of damaging the laptop though).

I even managed to be mobile with some of the active incomes I have earned. Many freelance positions pay on a per-unit basis. You complete the unit (write the article, edit the title, fix the whatsit) and return it to the company. When the item is approved your payment is scheduled. I could write articles and edit titles anywhere I had an active internet connection and frequently sat at the Riverfront when I worked. However, note that hourly active incomes may not be as flexible: they may require a certain computer, router configuration and a degree of silence that you may be unable to duplicate outside of the home. That said, some of my friends manage to meet requirements like these while on the road in hotel rooms and guest bedrooms.

How can I work with my kids underfoot?

It is a challenge but you will have to train your children to allow you to work. With babies this is impossible; you will have to work when they sleep or are with a sitter (or on a visit with family). As they get older you can teach them to play quietly while you work. You can start with just a few minutes at a time and increase the length as they mature.

The first computer Katie built to help Mommy.

When Katie was small I worked and studied while she was sleeping. Then I started bringing out my work while she was playing quietly. When she would ask I would explain what I was doing and tell her that she could help Mommy work by being quiet and playing. I would reward her with praise and quality time afterward.

As she got older I built an old computer from scraps and set it up at her level. I loaded it with age-specific programs and said that was her computer to work on while I did my work. The machine didn't cost anything and it was just an issue of time if I had to wipe it. When I would work on a client's computer she would get on hers and "buy eBay" or "check email" (her computer didn't even go online at the time) as she played her games. It made her feel like she was helping me and I praised her for working on her own computer quietly.

It was not perfect but over time she learned that if she allowed Mommy to work that I would read her a story, play a game or make a treat afterwards and she really loved her Mommy time. Many times, especially when she was younger, I had to stop working because I couldn't concentrate or properly supervise her but things got better as time went on.

We got to the point where I could take her on jobs to fix computers and even to restaurants while I worked. She learned to play quietly when I was studying and working. By the time I learned how to completely work online she was a pro: she would pull out her coloring materials then sit right beside me and draw while I spoke to customers. We learned how to sign to each other while I was on a call: On the phone I could help someone reset their whole network while I silently helped Katie with her homework.

Nowadays we tend to spend most of our time at the kitchen table. When we're not chatting or watching a movie together we are on our respective laptops. I'll be writing while she may be reading an ebook or playing a game. We sometimes go to the library, a restaurant or even a park with our laptops. She may browse the stacks, surf the net, read a book or otherwise amuse herself while I work but we always make time for just us to hang out, talk, take walks or whatever--especially now that I'm free to work (or not) as I choose.

Just as my daughter learned how to support me while I worked, your children will learn how to support you as well. Just stay calm and avoid getting upset when chaos happens (and it will). The upset only make things worse for everyone.

I have a boyfriend/husband. Why do I need to bother with this?

Because in this age relationships don't always last and it is better to be prepared financially than to discover yourself on the street with kids to feed and nothing to your name.

My boyfriend/husband doesn't want me to work. Should I do this anyway?

Yes. No one should force you to be dependent upon them. That is simply another form of slavery. If he wants you to "not work so much" that's great--eliminate the active income but never EVER quit building your passive income. Relationships don't always last anymore so you can't count on him being there forever. You may end up having to support the kids on your own before it is over with so build your passive income before you need it--even if you have to do it while he is at work or asleep or whatever.

This leads me to my cardinal rule: *Never* allow yourself to become financially dependent upon a man. This gives them a dangerous power over you. When they feel like they own you they will treat you more like a possession than a person and you may start hearing things like "if you don't like it, leave!" or threats to kick you and the kids out if you don't obey his wishes. Always have money of your own coming in--it is safer. That way if you or your children are ever abused by him you will have money of your own to leave him high and dry to start over and escape him.

Will I have to work ALL of the time?

If you are using active methods to generate income, yes. That is why I believe that building passive income is so important: You can't be truly free without it. That said, even when I was living on an active income I would take what

Tim Ferris calls mini-retirements; several months of traveling, sightseeing, visiting family and sitting on my butt while I enjoyed life with my kid.

Can I stop working for passive income?

I don't know. Theoretically it is possible but I've gotten to the point where I have so much fun writing that I've not stopped to find out. I have been known to take several months off between books (I'm not very productive in the summer) without issue. Back when I used to work for active income I would save enough money to live on for several months and take what Tim Ferris calls a mini-retirement. Those can be done easily enough, especially with passive income. You take this time to relax, decompress and take care of your family; choose another project and start again when you are ready. As for permanent retirement, I really don't know because I can't stop writing long enough to find out. If you keep building your passive income the sky is the limit on what you can make so why quit completely?

What about taxes?

There *will* be taxes you have to pay. I'm not a tax expert and my life is so simplified that I rarely have enough deductions to bother with but your situation may be different. Save all of your receipts (yes, you will need to keep records) and consult a tax professional about this subject.

What equipment do I need?

It depends upon what you decide to do. For instance, if you clean houses you will need cleaning equipment. If you work on computers you will need computer repair tools and software. If you want to rent out movies you will need a supply of movies to rent. If you want to rent storage space out, you will need the space to rent out. If you create music, you will need your instruments, a place to record, recording equipment (this can be as simple as a Mac laptop), a computer (if you don't have one for the recording) and an internet connection to upload your music to the distributor.

Writing requires at the minimum a laptop and an internet connection but you don't have to own either (see How to Write and Sell an Ebook[2] for details). I also use copious Post-it

---

[2] https://www.smashwords.com/books/view/36647

Notes, ink pens and notebooks to jot down notes and work through the planning stage but each writer is different in their creative process. I find that fooling with the physical notes helps me organize my thoughts better during the initial brainstorm stage of creation. If you are interested in writing books to generate your income I have written two volumes that teach about this: How to Write and Sell an Ebook[3], a primer for beginners that shows you how to write your first book even if you don't have a computer and How to Write Ebooks for a Living[4], which explains the steps I used to generate sufficient passive income from my books to become a stay at home single mother.

---

[3] For a complete list of my books and purchase information please visit http://annienygma.com/book-list/.

[4] https://www.smashwords.com/books/view/106806

Motivation

One of the biggest challenges (especially at the beginning) is staying motivated. When you first become a SAHM your friends and family may not understand what you are doing. Some may think you have lost your job or are pursuing other, more shady methods of income generation.

In order to motivate myself I collected news clippings of single mothers who accomplished my dream. I would spread them out around me and reread them when I needed the inspiration. My two favorite stories are about Eileen Goudge and J.K. Rowling; both ladies clawed their way off the welfare rolls to become wealthy, successful authors (and thus stay at home mothers).

I love drinking out of a coffee cup emblazoned with a motivational saying and looking up on my wall to a reminder to believe. I even decorate my laptop with small notes to inspire me. Some of these say: "I can do this and I do it," "I can do anything that I set my mind to," "whatever the mind can conceive and believe I will achieve," and "by golly, I can beat this!" They can really help when you get stuck at a rough patch.

Write down some of your favorite motivational sayings and stick them in random places in your home. I have them on my computer, the bathroom mirror, on the refrigerator and even in my van. Every time you discover a new saying that inspires you write it down and post it somewhere. These will help you get over the humps during the dark times.

If you find yourself battling depression you may want to jump start yourself by reading my book Be Happy Now[5]. It is hard to work when you are depressed but if you can change your focus you can use it as a huge catalyst to change your life for the better.

You will need to be dedicated and force yourself to work sometimes. It is especially hard to motivate yourself when you see dishes in the sink and laundry in the hamper but you will have to do this even though you *don't* have a boss breathing down your neck. One way I handled this at first was to take my kid to the park and work on my laptop while she played.

---

[5] http://annienygma.com/Be_Happy_Now.htm

This got me out of the house and away from the temptation to clean. We also went to the library where she would wander the stacks and play the games they had in the children's section while I would sit in a corner using the free internet to work while she had fun in safety.

On the days when I didn't have kids I would go to coffee shops, libraries, parks--even McDonalds--to work when the urge to clean instead of work became hard to resist.

I would imagine that the bills I owed were monsters breathing down my neck and that the only way to escape was to reach my quota for the day. I would sit down at the computer and not allow myself to take a break until I had an article finished and would not quit for the day until I reached my earnings quota. It was a challenge at first but it quickly became a habit. I would work as quickly as possible so that I could get on with my day.

Just remember: some progress is better than no progress at all. If you are able to do just one little thing each day toward your goals you *will* accomplish them. The only true failure is when you stop trying so don't ever allow yourself to quit. It is better to be the tortoise that slowly walks to the finish line than to be the rabbit who quits halfway through!

Simplify

The simpler your life the less you will have to deal with. The less you have to deal with, the more time/energy/money/focus you have for what you want to accomplish.

Think of your time, energy and money as the finite resources they are. You only have so much of these to go around no matter how you slice them up. When you allow all of your resources to be spent on the status quo then you won't have any available for improving your life.

You will need to make some time available so that you can regularly work on your goal of being a stay at home mom. This time will have to be borrowed from somewhere unless you have figured out how to add an extra hour to the day.[6] I share tips and information about

_____

[6] If you ever figure out how to do this please share it with me!

simplifying your life to achieve your dreams in the book <u>Minimize To Maximize</u>[7].

If you want to become a SAHM in record time you will need to reduce your financial obligations as well. This step is essential if you want to make the transition to SAHM fast and easy. The logic is this: it is much easier to earn $500 a month than it is to earn $5,000. My book <u>The Shoestring Girl: How I Live on Practically Nothing And YOU Can Too</u>[8] reveals the steps I use personally to keep my expenses extremely low.

I would not have been able to become a SAHM so easily if it were not for simplifying my life. It can make an astounding difference in the effort involved to achieve your goal.

---

[7] http://annienygma.com/Minimize_to_Maximize.htm

[8] http://annienygma.com/Shoestring_Girl.htm

Accept Help

Pride is not a good thing to have *especially* when you are first starting out. You may have to do things your old self may balk at. Lock your pride inside a sturdy box and bury him until you are a successful SAHM. After that you can bring him out to play with occasionally.

When you first start out (especially if you are single) you may discover that you qualify for help like Food Stamps (SNAP benefits), Medicaid, housing, cash payments, child support or even for some form of disability payment. You may have family who want to help you out while you get on your feet.

Accept this help and be grateful! Any assistance you receive means that you won't have to work quite as hard to produce active income and you will have more time and energy to pursue passive income.

If you are still married (or in a relationship) try to stay there until your passive income is enough to support you. The only exception to this rule would be if you are in an abusive relationship. If you are, escape as soon as possible and worry about money later. This may sound cold but it isn't just about you and your pride; it is about the children you are supporting as well.

When you become fully self-supporting you will wean yourself from this assistance. If the assistance comes from the government they will work with you as your income grows to the point where you no longer qualify for benefits. They will be especially helpful if you are honest about your goals and your income.

If you find yourself qualifying for medical benefits take advantage of this and have any medical checkups, eye exams and dental work done while you are able. Also make sure that your kids have their checkups and medical care as needed. You will perform better if you are healthy and rest easier knowing that you can take your kids to the doctor if they need it.

Money Talks

Congratulations, you have reached the heart of this book; how to make the money. This is the section that shows you how to have the bacon come to you without ever having to leave home.

Yes, it can be just that easy! I've been lazy in bed today as I work on this book but I'm still making money automagically.

There are two main forms of income we will cover here: Active and Passive income. Active income is just like any old job--you don't get paid if you don't work. Passive income is the magic that can change your life; the money that you receive whether you work or lay around in bed all day.

Of course, if your kids are small you may not be able to stay in bed *all* day. Unless you can persuade them to join you that is! I used to snuggle up with my Katie when she was a baby and watch television. As she became engrossed (and frequently dozed) I would take my laptop out and type away!

Active Income

Active income is any money that you receive in exchange for goods you make or services you perform. Jewelry making, crafts, babysitting, house cleaning, dog walking, article writing or the repair of computers and other items fall within the category of active income. To determine if something creates active income ask yourself if the money will continue coming in even after you stop doing (or making) the item/service in question. If the answer is no, it is active income.

Active income has several advantages. The pay can be quite sizable depending upon the work performed and is either immediate or arrives fairly soon after the job is completed. It is also the type of income most of us imagine when we think about paying the bills.

Active income has one serious disadvantage: When you stop working, the money stops coming. If you get sick, injured or for any reason are unable to perform the service or create/obtain the product your income will stop as well.

When you choose to pursue an active income select among the ones that allow you to work at home so that you can be close to your children. If you start your own business you can choose to take your children with you provided they are well-behaved. When I owned a computer repair business I would reward my children by allowing them to come to work with me. We would bring books, drawing materials and other items to amuse them while I worked on the clients' machines. Good behavior was rewarded with a treat at the end of the job.

I've even worked at restaurants where I could take my daughter with me. I had to work the night shift but my daughter was allowed to hang out in the office and break areas while I earned enough to pay our bills. Some smaller businesses will allow you to bring your well-behaved children to work as well. You may have to accept a lower cash payment in exchange for the privilege but you will save the money in babysitting expense (and know your child is safe with you instead of being exposed to predators).

The internet has drastically increased the opportunities for parents who wish to work at home. Websites like MTurk.com, Fiverr.com and others allow you to work when you are able to instead of on someone else's schedule. When I started working from home (aside from my computer repair business) I wrote articles, edited titles and even answered text messages while I learned how to generate the passive income that now gives me the freedom to do what I want when I want.

Some companies will hire you to do customer service and other work at a traditional hourly wage. One company I worked for was https://www.cloud10corp.com. The pay was good and you were able to choose the schedule that suited you.

Active income is a wonderful way to jump start your life as a stay-at-home parent. You are able to work at home and save money by eliminating the headaches associated with having to go elsewhere to work every day. If you've ever had a babysitter cancel at the last moment or a daycare refuse to take your child because she was ill you will immediately see the benefit to this.

If working on the internet intimidates you at first consider running a small business out of your home. You can clean houses, wash cars, groom/bathe pets, pet sit and even collect metals to recycle. I knew one lady who rented out her movie collection to earn enough money to open her first movie rental store! When you are ready to transition to online work, you can explore websites like fiverr.com to earn money doing simple tasks before branching out to the bigger stuff.

Many SAHMs enjoy active income so much that they never make the leap into earning passive income. If you feel this way that's okay! This is *your* life--live it in a way that pleases YOU. If you are content working at home keep doing it! However, if you are interested in freeing up your time so that you can do what you *want* to do, read on! I'll show you how to do that in the next section.

Passive Income

Passive income is any revenue that keeps coming in regardless of how you spend your time. No matter what you do (or don't do) you will still have money coming in once you have set up a passive income stream.

Interest and dividends are two classic examples of passive income. Regardless of whether you spend your time at the beach or crunching numbers, the interest on your investments will keep coming.

There are many more forms of passive income than you may know about. Not only is there interest and dividend investment income, there is advertising income (from web sites and other places--you can even sell advertising space on your car!), rental income (renting out rooms, movies, furniture and tools as well as real estate), drop shipping and information products.

Information selling is one of the easiest ways to develop passive income. All you have to do is share what you know in a format that is comfortable to you. You package this information and sell it to interested people. The best information products teach their recipients how to solve problems or accomplish goals-- like this one, that teaches you how to be a SAHM even if you're single.

You can write fiction, record music, make videos--whatever you are most comfortable with that you can package and sell. Once you create these products you can sell them again and again with almost NO effort on your part. That is where the passive part comes in.

For instance, I have written 18 books. Several are in print and the rest are in ebook format only. These books provide enough income for me to pay all of our bills and have money left over every month. I have been financially self-sufficient from my ebooks now for over a year and have written 4 more books (not including this one) since I reached the point where I knew I didn't have to take accept outside jobs to ensure that we had more than enough to meet our needs.

The best part about creating books (or music, or videos) is that the income from them builds up like money in the bank. Your first one may not sell very many copies in a month but add another and another to it and that income will multiply. Yes, even the flops will earn you money!

If you focus on one area where you are most comfortable (I focus on teaching others how to use simplicity and frugality as tools to achieve dreams and freedom) you can refer to your other works and guide your reader to more information on a particular section or subset without having to publish it all at once. This benefits your reader because they are not overwhelmed with information they may not be interested in and allows you to tailor your content to your readers and also generate a few more sales from those who may want more information about a particular area of your expertise.

The trick is not to *do* what you love, it is to *show people about what you love*; to show them how to do it is the heart of the information business. When you can solve a problem your information will always be in demand.

To summarize, passive income is the mother lode of the stay at home mother. Passive income is what will allow you to remove your focus from making money and apply it where you want--your family. It should be the goal of every parent to build sufficient passive income to live on before having kids in order to enjoy every youthful moment but most of us don't think ahead like that; I know I didn't.

Annie Jean Brewer

The one thing about passive income is that unless you win the lottery, inherit a lot of cash or write a bestseller straight off the bat you will have to build it up over time. The initial steps can be a significant amount of work but the payoff is a freedom that many work a lifetime to possess.

Which Should I Choose?

Since you may need an income instantly I recommend a combination of both active and passive income, with a goal to reduce and eventually eliminate the active income as the passive income increases.

This provides you the benefit of a near-instant income flow and the inspiration to work toward building your passive income. It is much harder to get inspired when your only income source is a single book that is only selling a couple of copies a month.

However, when you can write an article and get an instant $3-$10 bucks for it, your motivation level goes up significantly.

I switched from writing articles for various companies online to writing blog posts for variety but you can pick whatever interests you.

Remember, this is *your* life. While I make my living writing books your interests may be in tennis balls (which you could have drop-shipped), music (which you record or perhaps resell), movies (which you write or create) or something I've never even heard of! You may be fascinated by homemade eco-friendly diapers and want to design a site that focuses on that one item complete with reviews, ratings and drop-shipped products.

Anything is possible so I've deliberately left this book open-ended on the *how* part. I feel that I would be remiss if I didn't share the method I personally used to become a single SAHM (writing ebooks) but I don't want to beat you over the head with the details just in case you would rather watch paint dry then create so much as a grocery list.

For active income check out my book <u>Where to Work Online</u>. It has a huge list of jobs, covering everything from phone actors (and actresses) to writers to customer service reps to craft assembly, with everything in-between. If you find a subject in there that interests you explore the links inside of it and then search online (Google is an incredible friend) for similar work at home positions.

For passive income, first decide what you want to do to generate the income. If you like helping others, consider investing in sites like Microplace.com, where you can earn interest while helping others with small loans. If you like real estate, save up a couple of thousand dollars and purchase a used mobile home on a lot (go cheap with your first place to minimize risk and maximize return), clean it up and rent it out.

If you find drop-shipping to be of interest check out one of the many books online covering the subject, do your research and open a web site.

And (shameless plug here) if you want to write ebooks for a living you can learn how I do it in my two books How to Write and Sell an Ebook and How to Write Ebooks for a Living.

If you aren't sure what you want to do explore your online bookstore. There are a variety of free and low-cost manuals available about making money in every field imaginable; this will help you to decide before you start.

The Transition

As your passive income increases you can decrease the amount of active income you earn until eventually you can quit dealing with active income sources entirely. If you keep your sources available you can always go back to working for active income if you need extra money or get bored.

Warning: when you begin living on passive income you may feel very decadently rich in comparison to your associates who have to actually work for a living! To my surprise we felt this way despite starting out on a very limited income. Having the ability to arrange your life as YOU see fit can work wonders on your stress levels, your emotions and even your health.

Also, having the knowledge that you alone are in command of your future is quite empowering; I don't believe I will ever look at a man the same again now that I know I am perfectly capable of taking care of my family without one! That confidence will show on the outside as well, making you much more attractive to the male population. Fortunately you will have the self-assurance to be able to weed out the losers from the winners when you are ready to pursue a relationship along with the strength that comes with knowing that you will be okay if things don't work out.

Conclusion

It took me 8 years to learn how to become a full-time stay at home single mother. It took another year to just learn how to develop a passive income by selling information and a year past that to actually start living on it.

I have taken this decade of experience and distilled it into its' simplest form in hopes that you can accomplish in months what took me years. In fact, I am confident that you can do just that!

The hardest part of any new undertaking is blazing the initial trail. I have cleared out the brush; it is up to you to follow the path. There is no time limit on the journey; no one will be there to pick you up if you fall or to carry you when you get tired but at the end you will find a paradise that most work their whole lives to achieve: freedom.

I've got a cold drink waiting for when you arrive. Have you started the trip yet?

About the Author

Annie Jean Brewer combines minimalism with frugality to live her dream of being a stay at home *single* mother. She is the author of 18 books, several of which are Amazon bestsellers.

She currently lives in Central Kentucky with her daughter and a small menagerie of pets. She loves reading, taking long walks and fostering animals for a local rescue. You can discover more about her at Annienygma.com

Connect With Annie Online:

Official Website:
http://annienygma.com

Email:
annie@annienygma.com

Facebook:
http://www.facebook.com/annienygma

Smashwords:
http://www.smashwords.com/profile/view/
annienygma

Twitter:
http://www.twitter.com/annienygma

Yahoo! Contributor Network:
http://contributor.yahoo.com/user/404202/
annie_jean_brewer.html

ARE YOU OVERWHELMED?

Are you tired of working constantly, fighting constantly and never seeming to make any headway? Minimalism can offer a solution to your problems. By eliminating the nonessentials you can free your time, space and money for what YOU want in your life.

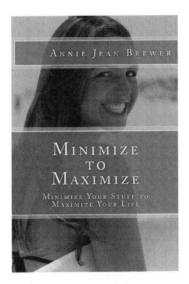

MINIMIZE YOUR STUFF TO MAXIMIZE YOUR LIFE!

WHY MINIMALISM?

Over a decade ago I found myself a single parent of three young daughters. After cramming as much of our stuff into a tiny mobile home that would fit, we put the rest in a storage building. Every week we would drive there, rotating items into and out of storage in order to just have enough room to breathe.

In those days the kids could demolish three rooms in the time it took me to clean one. It was a never-ending battle; I worked multiple jobs, went to school, cared for the kids but somehow I still had to find time to take care of our home. I was so completely exhausted that when friends even suggested I take some time off I became hostile; I desperately needed MORE time to do what needed to be done, not LESS!

One day in a fit of rage I started gathering up stuff and throwing it away. Oh my! The open space recharged me, inspired me to do even more. Boxes and bags and more ended up dumped at the curb on trash day and I came to a realization that changed my life:

The less I owned, the easier it was to clean.
The less I owned, the less there was to trip over.
The less we had, the less I had to work to pay for it!

Eventually I was able to pare down not only our possessions but our finances as well. This enabled me to pursue two of my most cherished dreams: that of a writer and that of a stay at home single mom. I purchased a mobile home in Western Kentucky and counted my blessings.

When my youngest daughter was taken from her elementary school by her father in late 2009 I used minimalism to focus upon what needed to be done to get her back.

In February of 2011 I took minimalism to the limit for this challenge. I gave almost everything we owned--mobile home, furniture, clothes and all--to a homeless woman, loaded up my an and drove away to get closer to my daughter and eliminate that drive.

Who Cares?

Your problems may be different but your situation is the same. You spend countless hours working and caring for things that really aren't important to you. Things you may or may not know if you can live without.

Things that you keep because you're afraid of what others will think if you get rid of them.

I know. I've been there.

I learned a lot of lessons in the decade I have studied and practiced minimalism. I have made mistakes and learned valuable lessons.

I have also gained a freedom that most only dream of, a freedom that would have been **impossible** without minimalism.

In this book you will discover:

✓ You don't have to deprive yourself in order to be a minimalist.
✓ There is no "wrong" or "right" type of minimalism.
✓ The advantages you experience when practicing minimalism.
✓ How to quiet the thoughts that are raging through your mind.
✓ The art of minimizing your commitments.
✓ How to increase your productivity.
✓ Five types of friends you should minimize your contact with.
✓ How to simplify your diet.
✓ Why you should minimize your finances.
✓ A risk-free way to minimize your possessions.
✓ Suggestions on minimizing your living space.
✓ How to maximize your dreams.

This book is born from real-life experience, designed to help you free yourself to achieve the goals that you desire without making the mistakes commonly made by newcomers to the minimalist movement.

Just as I have used minimalism to become a stay-at-home single   mother and bestselling author, you can use minimalism to achieve YOUR dreams.

DO YOU WANT TO ACHIEVE YOUR DREAMS?

Do You Want to Live on Less?

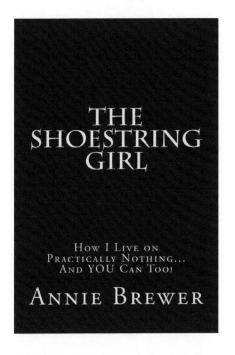

Would you like to learn how from someone who actually does?

Over ten years ago I found myself a single mother with three children to raise.

I had to learn fast.

I had to support those kids on a fast food paycheck while I put myself through school.

Not only did I manage to do it but I topped my own expectations. We ended up living better than I ever would have imagined.

Since then I have not only quit my day job but I have built up sufficient income to become a single stay-at-home mother to my youngest child. This feat would not have been possible without the frugality of shoestring living.

We live well on about $500 a month – and know how to live on even LESS!

Over the years I have shared my secrets with others who have fallen on hard times. I have helped friends who became disabled, single parents, the unemployed and others who found a need to live on as little money as possible.

The first thing I always shared was the timeless words of my grandmother. Even now I can hear her reminding me to hold up my head because...

"There's no sin in being poor!"

This may be your first brush with life below the poverty line. You may be scared. You may be ashamed. You may not know what to do or where to start.

I'm here to help you save money

I have drawn upon my 10+ years of personal experience to create the ultimate frugal living guide. I won't bore you with stupid fluff about clipping coupons. Instead, you will find a concise method you can implement to save thousands of dollars over the course of a year.

Sections Include:
Housing
Auto
Groceries (Includes raising food)
Computers (includes where to find free and
inexpensive software)
Television (includes watching shows online for
free)
Books (lots of links to free ebooks and how to
search for free ebooks online)
Music (includes links for free music sites)
Clothing
Cleaning tips and recipes
Personal care tips and recipes
Furniture
Thrift Shops
Yard Sales
Jobs and self-employment
And much more!

I not only explain the exact methods that I use
to save money and live frugally but I also
explain how I could live on about half of the
money that I actually do.

While you may not wish to apply everything
here I am confident that you will be inspired to
save more money than you ever thought

possible. You will learn the skills you need to overcome your current financial challenge.

Start Saving Money Today!

Do you Want to Earn a Living from Ebooks?

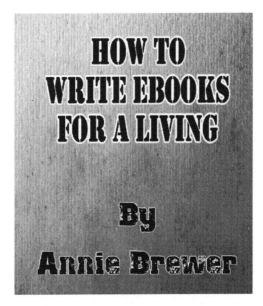

As a single mother I asked the question: How can I stay at home with my child but still pay the bills?

Job after job kept taking me away from my daughter's fleeting childhood. My frustration grew every time I missed another milestone in her life.

I combed the Internet in search of the answer. I found several places online where you could work from home but many of these kept me literally chained to a computer for hours on end. There had to be a better way!

One day I stumbled upon a blogger selling ebooks from his website. Not only selling them, he was actually earning his living from ebook sales!

"I can do that!" I thought.

I contacted him, buttered him up and picked his brain.

Gleefully following his instructions I finished my first ebook, published it online and drooled at the screen in anticipation.

I sat, I watched, I waited. After my first few sales the money dried up like a puddle in the desert.

What was I doing wrong?

I went out in search of more writers and picked a few more brains. I stayed up late at night researching and experimenting, determined to become a successful ebook writer. I refused to give up and quit.

I discovered the secret to ebook success.

Now I spend my days at home instead of at the dreaded day job. I take long walks with my daughter instead of punching a time clock. Money comes automatically now so I can relax and enjoy my life.

Anyone can make a living with ebooks,

GUARANTEED

If you follow the steps in this guide you are guaranteed to earn money with ebooks. I am so convinced that you will be able to earn a living entirely from ebook sales that I offer you a 6-month money-back guarantee. If after 6 months of applying this method you are not earning money from your ebooks send me a copy of your purchase receipt and I will refund your purchase price.

This guide teaches you:

What equipment you need to write ebooks
What bank accounts you need
How to financially prepare to live off your
ebook royalty income
Where to find the time to write
The importance of a blog
Where to practice writing in preparation
Where to find subjects to write about
How to create your ebook
Where and how to create an ebook cover
Ebook descriptions
Where to distribute your ebook
Ebook pricing
The importance of a backlist
Social media
Making the leap by quitting your day job
And more!

"A journey of a thousand miles begins with a single step." - Confucius.

Will you take that step today?

Do you want to work at home?

There are so many scams out there it is hard to determine legitimate work at home jobs. It took me years of searching and I stumbled upon my first legitimate opportunity entirely by chance.

Since then I have learned how to work entirely from home and have compiled a list of legitimate work at home opportunities. There is a little here for everyone as well as tips to avoid getting ripped off by the scams out there.

This book shows you:

The Golden Rule to working online
Money Matters
Multiple Income Streams
Fast Cash
Tinkering Cash
Searching Cash
Writing Cash
Therapy Cash
Affiliate Links
Roll Your Own (ebook that is..)
Phone Actresses
"Official" Jobs
Clearinghouses
The Big List of Online Jobs
And more!

If you are serious about working online, this is the only book you need.

"He that can live sparingly need not be rich."
Benjamin Franklin

There are a lot of frugality books out there.

I know. I've bought most of them.

Saving money isn't just a hobby for me; it is a way of life. It is what allows me to be a single stay-at-home mother for my child. We currently live on about $500 a month but if we wanted to we could easily live on less.

Here are just a few of the tips that I personally use to **save thousands of dollars** a year:

Tip #1 - Auto purchases. Annual Savings: $5,364.

Tip #32 - General Cleaning. Annual Savings: $216.

Tip #45 - Carpet cleaning. Annual Savings: $100.

Tip #67 - Salvaging stained clothing. Annual Savings: $50.

Tip #78 - Printer ink. Annual Savings: $100.

Tip #89 - Software. Annual Savings: $200

Tip #95 - Movies. Annual Savings: $52

Tip #100 - Television. Annual Savings: $1,200

Tip #114 - Credit Cards. Annual Savings: $480

Tip #129 - Where to work for Maximum savings. Annual savings: $1,011

Tip #241 - Housing. Annual Savings: $3,600

What could you do with that much extra money?

Written by the author of <u>The Shoestring Girl:</u>
<u>How I Live on Practically Nothing and You</u>
<u>Can Too</u>, this guide covers:

Auto
Cleaning
Computers
Entertainment
Finance
Food
Gardening
General Household
Housing
Kids
Personal Care
Pets
Shopping
Travel
Utilities
Funeral expenses
And more

Minus the fluff, this nitty-gritty guide
immediately gets down to the business of
saving money with over 400 unique tips
designed to help anyone with a desire to save
money.

You may not choose to use all of the frugal
ideas in this guide but I am confident that this

book will inspire you to save more money than you ever thought possible.

How Much Can YOU save?

Can You Afford Your Cable Bill?

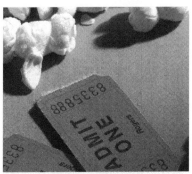

How to Watch
Movies and Television
Shows For Free
Annie Jean Brewer

When I left my abusive husband I had no job
and no money.

I had to think fast.

I had three bored kids in a tiny home all
screaming for entertainment.

I had to find a way to occupy those kids so that
I could focus on getting a job. I also needed to
distract myself as I struggled through a messy
divorce.

Desperate for a solution I tried everything looking for an answer to the question:

How do I watch television for free?

We tried antennas but the signal stank.

We borrowed movies but the selection ran out.

We even tried renting but you have to have money for that.

Late one night I sat crying at my computer. What type of mother couldn't even afford cable for her kids?

That's when it hit me.

Try the Internet.

I opened a browser and started searching. The web was still fairly new at the time but after some digging I hit paydirt.

Movies!

I made a few mistakes, crashed my computer and infected that machine more times than I can count. I strived to learn from those early days, driven by the fact that my family could now

Watch television for FREE!

Not only television but movies, webisodes, anime, documentaries, cartoons, trailers, tutorials and even more revealed themselves on my computer screen.

My kids became very happy after that.

I have crammed over a decade's worth of experience into this book. Within these pages you will find:

* How to prepare your computer system

* What software you need

* How to watch movies on your television

* A list of video websites

* Tips about registration

* Torrent and File Sharing Safety

* How to deal with pesky popups and ads

* How to view movies and shows

* How to find new video websites

* And more!

The tips and websites within this book are the very same ones that my family uses today. We watch whatever we desire and outside of our monthly internet bill we don't pay a single penny.

Wherever you are with your finances, chances are that you struggle to pay your bills at times. I've been there and I would like to make your entertainment expense less of a burden on your family.

Purchase this book today.

You can cancel your cable bill tomorrow.

When you are depressed, nothing seems to help.

I know, I've been there.

The day will come when you've finally had enough, when you are sick and tired of laying in your bed waiting for yet another day to pass. What will you do?

Most self-help books are so filled with fancy theories and trite advice that they forget the biggest problem that you are facing: You need something that works right now, something that will jump start your life.

Be Happy Now

Be Happy Now is the one book designed to help with immediate results. There is no fluff, no "expert opinions" and no Bullshit involved - just the exact methods I have used personally to overcome depression in my own life. Inside you will find:

• That the only one responsible for your happiness is you.

• How to create your personal Happiness Snowball and start it rolling downhill.

• How to exercise your atrophied Happiness muscle.

• Visualization techniques designed to allow you to mentally take control of your problems and vanquish them.

• How to keep those happy feelings you have gained.

Why Can I Trust You?

Just like you, I've battled depression. I've lain in bed while my kids tiptoed through the house whispering "Mommy is sick." I've felt even worse listening to them because I couldn't bring myself to get up, get dressed and take care of my precious babies.

I've been scolded by others who just didn't get it, who didn't understand my depression, who thought I was just being lazy, who didn't realize that they were actually making things worse.

My brain was so mushed that I couldn't focus on traditional methods to battle depression. I needed something simple to focus on.

This book contains the answer.

I used the tricks in this book to climb out of that deep, dark hole. I got out of that bed and, using the quick and dirty methods presented here not only overcame my depression but changed my life. Instead of feeling like a victim I took charge of my life and gained the courage to follow my dream of becoming a writer. Now I am living a life that others dream of - and I couldn't have done it without the first steps outlined in this book.

What this book is NOT:

This book is not a Depression database listing every single feel-good method available. This book lists the most basic, elementary steps designed to gently reprogram your mind to focus on the positive instead of the negative quicksand you are buried in.

This book is not based on theory. This stuff works.

This book is NOT designed to be a long read. It is designed to be a quick rope you toss to yourself or to a friend. It is designed to give you just enough to get started.

This book is NOT designed to overwhelm you. Most self-help books are filled with so much stuff that you think "oh, I can't do all that!" and they get set aside as a result. This book is short, sweet and designed for you to say "that's simple enough - I'll give it a shot."

What Do You Have To Lose Except Depression?

Please help others by reviewing this book. If you send me a link to your published review (my email address is annie@annienygma.com. I will be happy to send you a PDF copy of this book for you to print out or share with others.

Thank you for your support!

Printed in Great Britain
by Amazon